Seasonal Sermon
Outlines

SEASONAL SERMON OUTLINES

LeRoy Koopman

Baker Books
A Division of Baker Book House Co
Grand Rapids, Michigan 49516

Contents

The New Year

A Formula for Facing the Future

Scripture: Deuteronomy 29:16–29
Text: "The secret things belong to the Lord our God; but the things that are revealed belong to us and to our children for ever, that we may do all the words of this law" (Deut. 29:29).

Introduction
    A. The people of Israel were at a threshold.
        1. Behind them were:
            a. The promises to Abraham, Isaac, and Jacob.
            b. The deliverance from slavery.
            c. The golden calf, faithlessness, and grumbling.
        2. Before them was the promised land.
            a. A place of great promise and potential.
            b. A place of uncertainty and danger.
    B. We, too, stand at a threshold—not of a new land, but of a new year.
        1. Behind us are:
            a. God's provision of salvation.
            b. The experience of both hardship and providence.
            c. Sins, faithlessness, and grumbling.
        2. Before us are:
            a. Promises and potentials.
            b. Uncertainties and dangers (national, community, family, personal).
    C. We are much like the Israelites.
        1. Ready to march forward, yet fearful.
        2. God gives to us, as He gave to Israel, a formula for facing the future (see text).

I. First Part of the Formula: "The secret things belong to the Lord our God."
    A. The "secret things" are the things we don't know about.
        1. Events of nation and world.
        2. Future condition of our families.
        3. Our health, financial success, etc.
    B. These things "belong to God."
        1. They are for Him to know, not us.
            a. This is an act of mercy.

   b. "Let the day's own trouble be sufficient for the day" (Matt. 6:34).

  2. This does not mean God is personally responsible.

   a. Human error and sin play major roles.

   b. But God does know all things and permits hardship and trouble to enter our lives.

 C. First implication: don't be obsessed with looking into the future.

  1. Many in the secular world are preoccupied with astrological and psychic predictions.

  2. Many in the religious world are preoccupied with best-selling, conflicting interpretations of prophecy.

  3. The Christian can be as misguided as the non-Christian.

  4. The Bible is not meant to be a giant jigsaw puzzle.

 D. Second implication: if the future belongs to God, we should not worry about it.

  1. Some things are beyond our control and responsibility.

  2. "Which of you by being anxious can add one cubit to his span of life?" (Matt. 6:27).

  3. We waste time and energy worrying about things over which we have no power.

II. Second Part of the Formula: "The things that are revealed belong to us and to our children for ever, that we may do all the words of this law."

 A. We are not to assume for ourselves the things that belong to God.

 B. Neither are we to leave for God the things that belong to us.

  1. We are to make use of our brains and bodies.

  2. The things that belong to us are:

   a. Those things we know about and can do something about.

   b. Our response to the plain teaching of Scripture.

   c. Our concern for justice, love, and mercy.

  3. The phrase "Let go and let God" can be an evasion of responsibility.

 C. Israel failed in the things that belonged to her.

  1. God promised her the land.

  2. Because of disobedience, she was not allowed to keep it.

 D. Applications to life:

  1. We don't know whether we will die of cancer (hidden things belong to God), but we do know the effects of smoking (things that are revealed belong to us).

  2. We don't know how much rain will fall, but farmers know what seed, fertilizer, and care is best for growing.

3. We don't know how our children will turn out, but we do know our responsibilities to them.
4. We don't understand completely how Christ's death can save us, but we know we must believe.
5. We don't know what temptations we will face, but we have a responsibility to strengthen ourselves.
6. We don't know whether or not a certain person will accept Christ, but we know what our responsibility is to the unsaved.

E. Even in the things which belong to us, we are not alone.
1. "It is the Lord who goes before you; he will be with you, he will not fail you or forsake you; do not fear or be dismayed" (Deut. 31:8).
2. "Work out your own salvation with fear and trembling; for God is at work in you" (Phil. 2:12, 13).

Conclusion

Let this be our formula for the New Year: we will grasp eagerly the responsibilities of today, for these things belong to us; and we will leave for God the uncertain tomorrow, for that belongs to Him.

Communion

A Worldwide Celebration

Scripture: I Corinthians 10:14–22; John 3:16, 17
Text: "Because there is one bread, we who are many are one body, for we all partake of the one bread" (I Cor. 10:17).

Introduction
    A. Celebrations come in all shapes and sizes.
        1. Private wedding anniversaries.
        2. Family and class reunions.
        3. Small town carnivals.
        4. Ethnic celebrations.
        5. National independence days.
    B. One celebration is observed worldwide.
        1. By people of every race, nationality, and color.
        2. By rich and poor alike.
        3. Under the flags of almost every nation.
        4. This celebration is Communion, the Lord's Supper.

I. In This Celebration We Acknowledge a Worldwide Need: "All have sinned and fall short of the glory of God" (Rom. 3:23).
    A. We set aside all boastings and claims of superiority.
        1. Instead of claiming goodness, we seek mercy.
        2. We share a common humanity, and, hence, a common need.
    B. The evidence of sin is worldwide.
        1. Hatred and injustice know no boundaries.
        2. Every nation has a crime problem.
        3. Everywhere there is restlessness and revolt.
        4. Everywhere there are attempts at suppression, manipulation, and discrimination.
        5. In all nations people are probing for answers to their personal problems.
    C. As we partake of the Lord's Supper, let us confess our part in universal sinfulness.

II. In This Celebration We Rejoice in a Worldwide Love: "For God so loved the world that he gave his only Son..." (John 3:16).
    A. God established no boundaries for His love.

      1. The text doesn't say God loved the Jewish world, the Gentile world, or the white world.

      2. It doesn't say God loved the rich world, the poor world, or the middle-class world.

  B. God expresses His love in provisions and possibilities for material welfare.

      1. Bread and wine are samples of these provisions.

      2. They represent both the basics (bread) and the luxuries (wine) of God's material blessings.

  C. God also expressed His love in provisions for our spiritual welfare.

      1. No material provision can insure the life of the soul.

      2. Through the gift of His Son, God has provided:

        a. Forgiveness.

        b. New birth.

        c. Eternal life.

  D. As we partake of the Lord's Supper, let us again accept the love of God for our salvation.

III. In This Celebration We Express a Worldwide Fellowship: "Because there is one bread, we who are many are one body, for we all partake of the one bread" (I Cor. 10:17).

  A. Eating together is a symbol of unity.

      1. The common meal is a symbol of loyalty, love, friendship, and unity.

      2. If people were angry with each other, they would refuse to eat together.

  B. Unity is symbolized by one loaf.

      1. The custom was to pass the loaf of bread, with each person tearing off a piece.

      2. This "one bread" is Christ, in whom we all participate and find life.

  C. The passage envisions a great banquet table.

      1. Extending from Rome to Corinth, to Philippi, to Galatia, etc.

      2. Today: that table extends to Canada, Russia, China, Europe, Africa, Australia, South America, and every island of the sea.

      3. Some are eating hard brown bread; others are eating rice cakes or corn bread. Some are drinking wine from silver goblets; others are pouring the juice of tropical plants from earthen bowls. Some are dressed in fur coats; others wear hand-me-downs.

      4. But we are all one in Christ.

        a. What we have in common is more important than the cultural or racial differences which separate us.

        b. We have accepted the same love and believed in the same Lord; we are united in a common purpose and will share the same heaven.

D. Various attempts have been made to limit the table.
1. Biblical times:
    a. The Pharisees were critical of Jesus for eating with publicans (Luke 5:30).
    b. Peter found it difficult to accept Gentiles.
2. Similar attempts have been made throughout history.
    a. Discrimination in churches: special seating areas, closed membership, etc.
    b. Snubbing of people who are different—socially, culturally, or nationally.

E. As we partake of the Lord's Supper, let us make a new commitment to fully accept all of God's children.
1. Beginning in our own congregation.
2. Then extending to our community and the world.

Conclusion

A. Let us enthusiastically participate with millions of Christians in this gigantic and significant worldwide celebration.
1. We acknowledge a worldwide need.
2. We celebrate a worldwide love.
3. We express a worldwide fellowship.

Palm Sunday

Enthusiasm

Scripture: John 12:9–19
Text: "So they took branches of palm trees and went out to meet him, crying, 'Hosanna! Blessed is he who comes in the name of the Lord, even the King of Israel!'" (John 12:13).

Introduction: A Story of Enthusiasm
A. Jesus' followers were happy believers.
B. They wholeheartedly accepted Him as their king.
C. They demonstrated their enthusiasm.
  1. They cried out, "Hosanna! Blessed is he ..." (text).
  2. They tore down palm branches and waved them.
  3. They made a welcoming carpet on the road with their coats.
  4. They were probably called "fanatics" by curious on-lookers.

I. God Wants Enthusiasm
A. Examples of enthusiasm in Bible:
  1. The psalms are full of exclamation marks.
  2. The prophets were enthusiastic.
  3. The early church was enthusiastic (Acts 2:43–47).
  4. Paul said, "For if we are beside ourselves, it is for God" (II Cor. 5:13).
B. God is critical of those who have lost their enthusiasm.
  1. "I know your works: you are neither cold nor hot. Would that you were cold or hot! So, because you are lukewarm, and neither cold nor hot, I will spew you out of my mouth" (Rev. 3:15, 16).
  2. God prefers that we be "hot" (enthusiastic).
  3. His second choice is "cold" (antagonistic).
C. The Christian has many reasons to be enthusiastic.
  1. He can be enthusiastic about the past.
    a. What was evil is forgiven.
    b. What was good is not lost.
  2. He can be enthusiastic about the present.
    a. Member of world's greatest team.
    b. Involved in the world's greatest cause.
    c. Strengthened by the world's greatest power.
    d. Led by the world's greatest leader.

3. He can be enthusiastic about the future.
   a. The promise of eternal life.
   b. The final chapters of Revelation are the most enthusiastic words ever written.

D. It is important to keep our enthusiasm for Christ alive.
   1. Some who shouted "Hosanna!" may have shouted "Crucify him!" five days later.
   2. Some today have lost their enthusiasm for Christ.
      a. Most who make confession of faith do so enthusiastically.
      b. Many eventually lose that excitement.
      c. They often lose it slowly, almost imperceptibly.
      d. Gradually their joy, vibrancy, and faithfulness dwindles.
   3. Others have kept and increased their enthusiasm.
      a. They are still faithful, active, bubbling.
      b. They attract others to the faith by their spirit.
      c. Many have conquered discouragements and crises.

II. How to Keep Enthusiasm for Christ Alive

A. Begin with a genuine conversion experience.
   1. Some who joined in shouting "Hosanna!" may have had no real commitment; they were only caught up in the excitement of the day.
   2. Some religious experiences today are superficial.
      a. Peer pressure or parental pressure to be a Christian.
      b. Emotional excitement of evangelistic experience.
      c. Rebound from a bad experience (drugs, cults, etc).

B. Determine to keep enthusiasm alive.
   1. Much of our attitude is within our control.
   2. Enthusiasm takes genuine effort and self-discipline.

C. Keep close contact with Christ.
   1. "Abide in me, and I in you. As the branch cannot bear fruit by itself, unless it abides in the vine, neither can you, unless you abide in me" (John 15:4).
   2. Prayer, Bible study, and worship are valuable points of contact.

D. Open your life to the Holy Spirit.
   1. "Enthusiasm" comes from two Greek words, *en* (full of) and *theos* (God). It means "full of God."
   2. The Holy Spirit is God as He lives within us.
   3. Every Christian believer has the Holy Spirit.
      a. "Repent, and be baptized every one of you in the name of Jesus Christ for the forgiveness of your sins;

and you shall receive the gift of the Holy Spirit''
(Acts 2:38).

    b. Each of us has great potential for enthusiasm.

4. We are to give the Spirit full freedom in our lives.

    a. ''Do not get drunk with wine . . . but be filled with the Spirit'' (Eph. 5:18).

    b. Open every aspect of life to His presence and control.

E. Channel enthusiasm into an avenue of service.

    1. Emotionalism seeks to be an end in itself.

    2. True emotion seeks to express itself in some concrete way and leads to action.

Conclusion

A. Today we join the crowds in Jerusalem, shouting ''Hosanna!''

B. A month from now, a year from now, a decade from now, an eternity from now, may you still have that enthusiasm for Christ the King.

Easter

Easter Dawns on a Troubled World

Scripture: Luke 24:1-16

Text: "But on the first day of the week, at early dawn, they went to the tomb, taking the spices which they had prepared" (Luke 24:1).

I. The First Easter Dawned on a World of Trouble
    A. The world was troubled.
        1. Jews were under the heel of Rome.
        2. Five million people were slaves.
        3. The rulers were more despotic than ever.
        4. The infant mortality rate was high; few lived to the age of six.
        5. Plagues swept unchecked through the population.
        6. Taxation was a great burden.
    B. Individuals were troubled.
        1. People wept and worried.
        2. Among them were friends of Jesus:
            a. Women wept as they prepared spices.
            b. Two men were sorrowful on the way to Emmaus.
            c. The eleven disciples were confused and disillusioned.

II. Easter Dawns on a World of Trouble Today
    A. The world is troubled.
        1. A few items from this morning's headlines: in the U.S. from 6 P.M. to 6 A.M. there were 27 murders, 29 suicides, 1,100 assaults and rapes, 70 killed in automobile accidents, and 10 million people drunk.
    B. Individuals are troubled.
        1. Many are anxious, depressed, and guilt-ridden.
        2. Many are worried about finances and concerned about children.
        3. They mourn the deaths of loved ones and friends.
        4. Some are slaves to drugs, alcohol, crime, or anger.

III. In a Sense, Easter Doesn't Change the World
    A. The world then:
        1. Rome kept on ruling; Jews kept on rebelling.
        2. Muscular men kept on whipping galley slaves.
        3. Gladiators continued to "entertain."
        4. People kept dying.
    B. The world now:

1. There is no instant cure for the world's ills. The same headlines appear day after day.

IV. Yet, Easter Does Change Some Things
A. The changes then:
   1. The women who trudged to the tomb raced back excitedly.
   2. The two followers who trudged to Emmaus recognized the risen Christ.
   3. The eleven disciples became bold fearless men, willing to die for a great cause.
   4. Some years later gladiatorial combat was banned at Rome's arenas.
   5. In A.D. 312 Constantine, a Christian, ruled the Roman Empire.
B. The changes now:
   1. People still mourn, but not without hope.
      a. "That you may not grieve as others do who have no hope" (I Thess. 4:13).
      b. "O death, where is thy victory? O death, where is thy sting?" (I Cor. 15:55).
      c. Christ guarantees the resurrection of those who believe in Him.
   2. The risen Christ still changes people.
      a. "If any one is in Christ, he is a new creation" (II Cor. 5:17).
      b. Spiritual rebirth changes ambitions, morals, lifestyles, attitudes, and inner beings.
   3. Easter is not just something we dress up for; it is the essence of hope.
      a. Hope for the drug addict and alcoholic.
      b. Hope for the troubled marriage.
      c. Hope for the person filled with hate.
      d. Hope for the grieving parent, husband, wife, child, and friend.
   4. Christian believers are in a position to help change their world.
      a. They can bring the witness of Christ to poverty and injustice.
      b. They can bring the spirit of the living Christ into business, government, the entertainment world, etc.

Conclusion
A. Easter dawns once more on a troubled world.
B. In one sense, the world will go on being troubled.
C. But for those transformed by the living Christ, the world has drastically changed and will continue to change.

Ascension Day

Space Travel?

Scripture: Acts 1:1–14
Text: "And when he had said this, as they were looking on, he was lifted up, and a cloud took him out of their sight" (Acts 1:9).

Introduction

    A. Space flight Apollo 10 lifted off on May 18, 1969—which, by remarkable coincidence, was Ascension Sunday.

    B. This brings us to an interesting question: Was Jesus' ascension something like the ascension of the rocket (which some people also might look on as a "savior")?

I. The Difficulty of Understanding the Ascension

    A. The difficulty of a simple interpretation—a body lifting from earth and zooming into space.

        1. Where is "up" on a spinning globe?

        2. Did He have to break the sound barrier?

        3. Did He leave the earth's atmosphere?

        4. Did He fly out past the moon, planets, and sun?

        5. Where in the solar system—or another galaxy—did He land?

    B. The difficulty of a symbolic poetic interpretation (the disciples had an "inner experience" only).

        1. The story is reported as history.

        2. The event caused a change in the disciples.

        3. Eleven people having the same hallucination at once is unlikely.

II. Some Considerations Which May Help Us Understand

    A. The nature of the incarnation.

        1. We don't try to figure out how many years it took Jesus to get here.

        2. Rather, Jesus descended from a mode of spiritual existence to a mode of material existence.

    B. The nature of Jesus' resurrected body.

        1. Jesus had already passed into a new mode of being.

        2. At times He became sufficiently material to be recognizable.

        3. Yet, He could appear and disappear from sight (upper room, Emmaus, etc.).

        4. He was no longer bound by earth's laws of space, time, or gravity.

5. He was no longer adapted to earth's mode of being.
C. Jesus' body didn't have to zoom like a rocket because it was no longer a material body.
1. By means of resurrection He had already conquered the limitations of time and space.
2. A rocketlike departure would have been a reversion to the former material existence.
3. Jesus' resurrected nature simply took its natural course and departed from earthly existence.
D. Yet, the disciples participated in a real event.
1. Jesus actually rose in the air, visibly, until a cloud took Him out of their sight.
2. He did so, not because He had to, but because of its educational value for the disciples.
a. Many times since the resurrection Jesus had disappeared and reappeared.
b. The disciples had to realize that this was final; He would walk with them no more.
3. His ascension was symbolic and real at the same time.

III. The Significance of the Ascension
A. It convinced the disciples of the real nature of the kingdom.
1. Even after the resurrection they asked Him, "Lord, will you at this time restore the kingdom to Israel?" (Acts 1:6).
2. Jesus now made clear that His reign was a spiritual one.
B. It made way for the era of the Spirit.
1. The man Christ was subject to the limits of time and space.
2. Now, through the Spirit, Christ can speak to all people in all places—including us.
C. Christ gives joy to believers.
1. "And they returned to Jerusalem with great joy" (Luke 24:52).
2. The ascension can give us joy.
a. The joy of Jesus' triumph.
b. The joy of a sympathetic heaven (see Heb. 10:19–22).
D. It gives us a glimpse of our own resurrection.
1. He will return to take us to Himself.
2. We, too, will enter a new reality, a new mode of life.

Conclusion
A. We may never get to ride in a rocket like Apollo 10.
B. But, by being one of Christ's people, we can share the secret of His resurrection and ascension and can "travel" from this earthly mode of being to a heavenly one.

Pentecost

Twelve Characteristics of a Spirit-filled Church (A Series of Sermons)

Scripture: Acts 2:37–47

Introduction
- A. The early church was far from a perfect church.
- B. Yet the early church had great vitality.
  1. It grew inwardly and outwardly.
  2. It pulsated with energy.
- C. Reason: it was filled with the Holy Spirit.
  1. Pentecost had just taken place.
  2. Peter had promised the Holy Spirit to every believer.
- D. Today we will point out twelve characteristics of that church.
  1. We believe a Spirit-filled church can happen today.
  2. God's Spirit is still alive and well.
  3. Advance warning: this is a twelve-point sermon!

I. The Members Are Genuinely Converted
- A. "So those who received his word were baptized, and there were added that day about three thousand souls" (v. 41).
  1. "Received"—means believed, accepted.
  2. "His word"—the gospel.
  3. Baptism—the symbol of cleansing by Christ.
- B. The motive for becoming a member is crucial.
  1. The motive should not be prestige, peer pressure, or opportunity to do good works.
  2. The motive should be genuine repentance and faith.

II. The Members Want to Be Taught the Truth
- A. "And they devoted themselves to the apostles' teaching" (v. 42a).
  1. After Jesus left the apostles had authority to teach.
  2. Their teaching was written down in the Gospels.
- B. Two lessons for us:
  1. The importance of accepting an authority for the practice of faith.
  2. The importance of continuing to learn and grow.

III. The Members Mix Socially with Other Christians
- A. "And they devoted themselves to the apostles" . . . fellowship, to the breaking of bread . . ." (v. 42).

        1. The common meal was a sign of fellowship and love.

  B. Let us seek the company of other Christians.

        1. We build each other up in the faith by sharing, encouraging, and being friends.

IV. The Members Regularly Observe the Lord's Supper

  A. "And they devoted themselves . . . to the breaking of bread . . ." (v.42).

        1. In the early church, not much distinction was made between the sacrament and the common meal.

        2. Perhaps they first held "potluck," then concluded with the sacrament.

  B. Let us participate often in the sacrament.

        1. Perhaps more informally, as in the early church.

        2. With a genuine sense of togetherness.

V. The Members Are People of Prayer

  A. ". . . and the prayers" (v. 42).

        1. This implies both private and public prayer.

        2. Devotional life is the doorway to God's Spirit.

  B. Let us maintain our vitality through prayer.

        1. Make it an integral part of each day's activities.

        2. Keep in constant touch with God.

VI. The Members Have a Sense of Awe

  A. "And fear came upon every soul" (v. 43a).

        1. "Fear" means to be amazed by, not afraid of.

        2. They were filled with awe by the wonderful things that were happening.

  B. Does your faith have a sense of wonderment?

        1. It's possible for religion to become tepid.

        2. Allow the Holy Spirit to create new experiences.

VII. The Members Experience Miracles

  A. "And many wonders and signs were done through the apostles" (v. 43b).

        1. The supernatural made itself evident.

        2. Acts 3, 5, and 9 record some of these miracles.

  B. We should expect miracles.

        1. Many churches would be surprised if a miracle happened.

        2. The Holy Spirit is alive; don't limit His power.

VIII. The Members Are Generous

  A. "And all who believed were together and had all things in common; and they sold their possessions and goods and distributed them to all, as any had need" (vv. 44, 45).

        1. This Christian "communism" was soon abandoned.

        2. But the motive was commendable.

B. The Holy Spirit moves people to be generous.
   1. Sense of stewardship: all belongs to God.
   2. Motive of love: seek the welfare of others.

IX. The Members Worship Together
A. "And day by day, attending the temple together . . ." (v. 46a).
   1. They didn't have their own church building.
   2. But they believed in the importance of public worship.
B. Public worship is still important today.
   1. Non-attendance is usually a sign of disinterest.
   2. Spirit-filled people want to go to church.

X. The Members Display Enthusiasm
A. "They partook of food with glad and generous hearts, praising God . . ." (vv. 46b, 47a).
   1. They enjoyed their faith.
   2. They regarded their faith as a privilege, not a burden.
B. Our religion is often too sober.
   1. We sometimes judge sincerity by somberness.
   2. We have much to be happy about!

XI. The Members Earn a Good Reputation in the Community
A. "And having favor with all the people" (v. 47b).
B. It is important to maintain good relationships.
   1. We should be neither morally loose nor insufferably pious.
   2. Our lives should be consistent with our words.

XII. The Membership Increases
A. "And the Lord added to their number day by day those who were being saved" (v. 47c).
   1. Growth was not monthly or weekly, but daily.
   2. "The Lord added" implies genuine commitment.
B. A Spirit-filled church is a growing church.
   1. Outsiders are attracted by the life and vitality.
   2. Outsiders see a church that meets their needs.

Conclusion
A. Twelve characteristics of a Spirit-filled church.
   1. The members are genuinely converted.
   2. The members want to be taught the truth.
   3. The members mix socially with other Christians.
   4. The members regularly observe the Lord's Supper.
   5. The members are people of prayer.
   6. The members have a sense of awe.
   7. The members experience miracles.
   8. The members are generous.

9. The members worship together.
10. The members display enthusiasm.
11. The members earn a good reputation in the community.
12. The membership increases.

Reformation Day

Tradition: Coping with the Past

Scripture: Matthew 15:1–9
Text: "And why do you transgress the commandment of God for the sake of your tradition?" (Matt. 15:3).

Introduction

    A. When we use the word *coping,* we usually use it in reference to the present or future.
       1. "Coping with change."
       2. "Coping with a crisis."
    B. On this Reformation Sunday, however, we ought to be reminded that it's also a challenge to cope with the past.
    C. We will examine the subject of coping with our tradition, especially our religious tradition, our spiritual heritage.

I. Tradition Is Often Harmful

    A. Biblical references to tradition:
       1. Negative aspects of tradition: Matthew 15:1–3, 7, 8; Galatians 1:14
       2. Positive aspects of tradition: II Thessalonians 2:15.
    B. Tradition is harmful when it is the tradition of people rather than of God.
       1. "Why do you transgress the commandment of God for the sake of your tradition?" (Matt. 15:3). "In vain do they worship me, teaching as doctrines the precepts of men" (15:9).
       2. Prior to the Reformation human traditions had crept into the church.
          a. A.D. 593—Purgatory.
          b. A.D. 1215—Transubstantiation.
       3. The purpose of the Reformation was to return to the Word, alone, as the guide for faith and practice.
       4. Since the Reformation, Protestants have added a great many of their own traditions, several of them rooted in culture rather than the Word.
    C. Even a good tradition can be harmful when it becomes an excuse for not showing love.
       1. Matthew 15:5, 6 refers to a traditional oath to give money to God—which became an excuse for not supporting aged parents.

2. Jesus said, "So for the sake of your tradition, you have made void the word of God" (v. 6).
3. Sometimes in enforcing the rules and maintaining discipline, we fail to obey the commandment to love.
   a. As parents.
   b. As a church.
   c. As a society.
D. Even a good tradition can be harmful if it becomes a mere form.
   1. "This people honors me with their lips, but their heart is far from me" (Matt. 15:8).
   2. See II Timothy 3:5.
   3. Some examples:
      a. Baptism can be merely a form.
      b. Church membership can be merely a form.
      c. Worship and prayers can be merely a form.
   4. Harmful traditionalism is adhering to the practices of the past without truly making them your own.

II. How to Guard Against Harmful Traditionalism
A. The church must always be reforming.
   1. The Reformation was a good start, but it was only a start.
   2. Traditionalism keeps creeping in like weeds into a garden.
   3. We must continually hold our faith and life before the mirror of Scripture.
B. We must strive to capture the spirit as well as the form of our religious acts.
   1. Come to church expectantly.
   2. Give the Holy Spirit room to move around.
   3. Be flexible regarding the forms and style of religious expression.
C. We must make our faith our own.
   1. We must not be content with the faith of our ancestors.
   2. We should refrain from going through the forms until there is an inner transformation.

Conclusion
A. In a sense, the Reformation is history; we celebrate it as a victory over tradition gone sour.
B. But, in a greater sense, the Reformation must continue, or others will view our faith as a tradition gone sour.

Mothers' Day

Beauty Is Heart Deep

Scripture: I Peter 3:1–6

Text: "Let not yours be the outward adorning with braiding of hair, decoration of gold, and wearing of fine clothing, but let it be the hidden person of the heart with the imperishable jewel of a gentle and quiet spirit, which in God's sight is very precious" (I Peter 3:3, 4).

Introduction

    A. Nearly every person wants to be beautiful.
       1. Whether age sixteen or sixty.
       2. Whether single or married.
    B. That ambition is commendable.
       1. It is good to strive for improvement and a pleasant appearance.
    C. Surprisingly, the goal of beauty is within the reach of every person.
    D. There are three ways to be beautiful:
       1. To be born beautiful.
       2. To buy beauty.
       3. To become beautiful.

I. Being Born Beautiful

    A. With some, beauty is a natural physical endowment.
    B. The Bible mentions women of extraordinary beauty.
       1. Sarah.
       2. Esther.
       3. The lover in the Song of Solomon (explicit references to her face and figure).
    C. Beauty can be a mixed blessing.
       1. *Notable Women in History* by Willis J. Abbot contains short biographies of seventy-three women, of whom twenty-nine are ranked as beautiful. Of these, eighteen met violent deaths.
       2. Surveys have indicated that beautiful women have more personal problems and unhappiness than plainer ones.

II. Buying Beauty

    A. Americans spend billions each year on cosmetics and clothing.
       1. Cosmetics are among the most highly-advertised products.

B. Buying beauty is nothing new.
   1. Our text mentions "outward adorning."
   2. Beauty aids around the world offer interesting variations.
      a. Hair: braided, loose, long, short, wigs.
      b. Skin: painted dark, white, red, yellow; scarred with decorative welts.
      c. Teeth: blackened, whitened, filed to a point, filed to the gum line.
      d. Lips: painted red, blue, purple; elongated.
C. Buying beauty has disadvantages.
   1. Expensive.
   2. Fads quickly change.
   3. Always superficial.
   4. Doesn't fool those closest to you.
D. Some interpret our text as condemning all such outward adornment.
   1. But saintliness is not synonymous with ugliness, poor grooming, or out-of-style fashions.
   2. The text points out relative values rather than giving absolute condemnation.

III. Becoming Beautiful
A. "But let it [your beauty] be the hidden person of the heart" (v. 4).
   1. "Your beauty should not be dependent on an elaborate coiffure, or on the wearing of jewelry or fine clothes, but on the inner personality" (Phillips).
   2. "Your beauty should reside, not in outward adornment . . . but in the inmost centre of your being" (NEB).
   3. In other words, beauty is heart deep.
      a. You can't be born with real beauty.
      b. You can't buy it.
      c. You can only become it.
   4. A plain face can be transformed by an inner light.
B. This is the beauty that really counts.
   1. A fourth grade teacher assigned students to write an essay, "My mother is . . ." A consistent result was, "My mother is beautiful." A visual survey showed little correlation between the physical beauty of mothers and their children's opinions. Children respond to warmth, security, and acceptance, which is beautiful to them.
   2. Our opinions of people should depend more on what they are than on what they look like.
C. How this beauty became a reality.
   1. We were created beautiful, in God's image.
   2. Sin destroyed that beauty; so transformation is needed.

3. Through Christ this transformation can take place.
   a. "You must be born anew" (John 3:7).
   b. "If any one is in Christ, he is a new creation; the old has passed away, behold, the new has come" (II Cor. 5:17).
4. Christ doesn't change our nose, figure, etc., but He changes our inner being.
5. This becomes increasingly true as more of our character and personality yields to Him. ("Let the beauty of Jesus be seen in me.")

D. The qualities of beauty.
   1. Reverence (v. 2a).
      a. Godliness.
      b. Acceptance of Christ.
      c. Loving regard for God and all His creatures.
   2. Chastity (v. 2b).
      a. Faithfulness to spouse.
      b. Judicious in all talk, conduct, and appearance.
   3. "A gentle and quiet spirit" (v. 4).
      a. This doesn't mean being without opinions, a doormat.
      b. It does mean having an even temperament, patience, loving disposition, humor, and affection.
      c. In a world of brashness and strife, Christians can provide sensitivity and tenderness.

E. This beauty will never fade.
   1. Natural beauty will diminish with age.
   2. Inner beauty can continue to improve.
   3. God's standard of beauty is never out of style.

Conclusion

Let us give God the praise for all those who have become beautiful in the Lord, who have captured the essence of the inner beauty of the heart.

Fathers' Day

The Visible Father

Scripture: Joshua 24:1–15

Text: "And if you be unwilling to serve the Lord, choose this day whom you will serve, whether the gods your fathers served in the region beyond the River, or the gods of the Amorites in whose land you dwell; but as for me and my house, we will serve the Lord" (Josh. 24:15).

Introduction

    A. In many ways, men have traditionally been more visible on the employment scene than women.

        1. Men are visible in factories, businesses, offices, armed forces, courts, government, and almost every area of life.

        2. Women were more often found working in the home and were less prominent in other areas of employment.

        3. This is a situation which many are trying to correct.

    B. In the role of parent, however, many men have been considerably less visible than women.

        1. They may be "invisible" because of divorce or separation.

        2. They may be "invisible" because of excessive involvement in work and play.

            a. Absorbed in job, community projects, and conventions.

            b. Recreation: "out with the boys."

        3. They may be "invisible" because they do not care to get involved in the responsibilities of being fathers.

    C. This "invisibility" is most evident in the area of spiritual leadership.

        1. Many fathers are not interested.

        2. Mothers must assume the responsibility for the religious training of children.

    D. Over against that trend, we hold up the example of Joshua, a very visible father.

        1. He was very visible as a military leader of Israel.

        2. He was also very visible as a spiritual leader in his own household.

I. The Visible Father Believes in a Basic Standard of Morality and Religious Dedication

    A. Joshua called for a decision: "choose this day whom you will serve."

        1. He didn't believe in making up rules as he went along.

2. He believed there must be basic commitments and principles.
3. He recognized the need for far-reaching decisions on the national and home level.
   B. Let us support and honor fathers who, like Joshua, maintain a basic standard of faith and life.
1. Who have made a commitment to Christ and who live by that commitment.
2. Who can distinguish between passing fads and eternal values.
3. Who demand that basic ideals be adhered to in government, business, and the home.

II. The Visible Father Makes Unpopular Choices
   A. Joshua was willing to take an unpopular stand ("choose this day whom you will serve . . . but as for me . . .").
1. His choice was already made; it was not dependent on theirs.
2. His decision was not determined by majority vote.
3. He was willing, if necessary, to stand alone.
   B. Today's "visible" Christian man may stand alone.
1. There is much pressure to conform to the standards of the world.
2. If he goes to church, he is in the minority.
   C. Let us support and honor fathers (and non-fathers) who are visible Christians, no matter what others do.

III. The Visible Father Makes Choices for Himself and His Family
   A. He makes no religious decision for himself without including his family ("as for me and my house").
1. He assumed spiritual responsibility for his family.
2. In many families, this is left to the wife.
3. In other families, this is left to the children.
4. God has delegated spiritual responsibility to both parents.
   B. He makes no religious decision for his family without involving himself (included "me" with "my house").
1. The visible father shows as well as teaches, takes to church as well as sends.
2. He makes a personal Christian commitment, then invites others to follow.
3. He makes every effort to be at home with his wife and children—leading, guiding, and counseling.

Conclusion
Let us honor those fathers who are "visible"—as wage-earners, as leaders in their communities, but especially, as loving and firm spiritual heads of their households.

Graduation

Dare to Be Great

Scripture: Matthew 20:17–28
Text: "Whoever would be great among you must be your servant, and whoever would be first among you must be your slave" (Matt. 20:27, 28).

Introduction
    A. One of the most popular subjects of books today is how to be great, how to be "number one," how to look out for yourself.
    B. That same theme is also popular among Christian writers and preachers.
    C. One of the early harbingers of this theme in the early 1970s was an Orlando businessman.
        1. He owned a cosmetics firm and dozens of other enterprises.
        2. He promoted and taught a course on how to be great.
        3. His slogan was, "Dare to Be Great."
        4. Unfortunately, he was convicted of fraud and related charges in Germany and the United States.
    D. Our Scripture story is about two men who dared to be great.
        1. They wanted to be at the "right hand" and "left hand" of Christ in His kingdom.
        2. The request was made by their mother Salome, the sister of Jesus' mother Mary.
        3. Jesus reproved them—not because their ambition was wrong, but because their standard was wrong (see text).

I. True Greatness Is Serving Rather Than Being Served
    A. The commonly accepted standard of greatness:
        1. Being served and honored by others.
        2. Being acknowledged as number one.
        3. Achieving first place, the highest score, the top office, the best position.
        4. Making the most money, buying the most expensive home or car.
        5. Power, prestige, and independence from others.
    B. Jesus' standard of greatness differs from this one.
        1. More emphasis on giving than on getting.
        2. More important to serve than to be served.

3. What we are is more vital than what we have.

4. Our stature is more significant than our status.

C. Jesus taught this standard by His words.

  1. Observations at the treasury (Mark 12:41–44):

    a. Some tried to achieve greatness by the amount of money they gave.

    b. The widow was great because of her degree of dedication.

  2. Parable of the Good Samaritan (Luke 10:29–37).

    a. The Jewish religious leaders were regarded as great because of their position.

    b. The theologically incorrect Samaritan was great because he served.

D. Jesus taught this standard by His deeds.

  1. "The Son of man came not to be served but to serve" (v. 28a).

    a. All His miracles were designed to help and to heal.

  2. "And to give his life as a ransom for many" (v. 28b).

    a. "Ransom"—payment for release of captives.

    b. Jesus made the greatest sacrifice possible.

II. The Advantages of Jesus' Standard of Greatness

A. Everyone can succeed.

  1. By the world's standard, only a few will succeed and the rest will fail.

  2. By Jesus' standard, everyone here can live a truly great and significant life.

B. We can be free from the tyranny of things.

  1. Possessions—and our anticipated possessions—can be terrible tyrants.

    a. People have sacrificed husbands, wives, children, friends, and themselves for possessions.

    b. They have used every questionable method to attain them.

  2. Jesus' standard of greatness frees us from this tyranny and places us under the Lordship of the one who came to serve.

C. We can be truly fulfilled.

  1. "Success," by the world's standard, seldom brings inner peace and satisfaction.

    a. It is based on superficial, passing things.

    b. It may meet the needs of body, but not of soul.

  2. Success, by Jesus' standard, brings the warmth of love and the confidence of a life well lived (John 10:10).

Conclusion

Graduates, dare to be great, but make sure you strive to be truly great.

Independence Day

The Price of Freedom

Scripture: Hebrews 11:23-40
Text: "Others suffered mocking and scourging, and even chains and imprisonment. They were stoned, they were sawn in two, they were killed with the sword; they went about in skins of sheep and goats, destitute, afflicted, ill-treated" (Heb. 11:36, 37).

Introduction
    A. As this sermon title implies, freedom is never free.
        1. Always bought with a price.
        2. Always maintained by a struggle.
    B. We will think in terms of three freedoms:
        1. Political freedom.
        2. Religious freedom.
        3. Spiritual freedom.

I. The Price of Political Freedom
    A. Moses, the liberator, paid a price (vv. 23-27).
        1. He gave up the luxury of a palace and left Egypt.
        2. He lived forty years in the wilderness.
    B. Other Old Testament heroes also paid a price for freedom (vv. 35-38).
    C. America, too, has paid a price.
        1. Revolutionary War—4,435 killed.
        2. War of 1812—2,260 killed.
        3. Mexican War—1,733 killed.
        4. Civil War—Union: 364,511 killed; Confederacy: 258,000 killed.
        5. Spanish American War—2,446 killed.
        6. World War I—116,516 killed.
        7. World War II—405,399 killed.
        8. Korean War—54,246 killed.
        9. War in Indochina—48,000 killed.
    D. There are many among us who have paid a great price for political freedom.

II. The Price of Religious Freedom
    A. Definition: the freedom to practice one's faith according to the dictates of one's own conscience.
    B. The early church.
        1. Stephen, the first martyr (Acts 7:54-60).

2. Paul (II Cor. 11:23–27).
3. Persecution of early Christians.
C. Religious persecution throughout history:
    1. Albigenses:
        a. A Christian sect in Albi, southern France, during the twelfth and thirteenth centuries.
        b. Critical of Catholic priests, believed matter is evil.
        c. The city of Bezieres was besieged and 30,000 were slain for providing asylum to fugitives of the sect.
    2. Waldenses:
        a. German reform group, twelfth century.
        b. Believed in Scripture alone; wanted Bible in their language; denied purgatory.
        c. Lands laid waste; homes burned; suffocated by fire when they hid in caves.
    3. Early reformers burned at stake:
        a. John Huss, Bohemia, 1415.
        b. Jerome of Prague, Bohemia, 1416.
        c. Jerome Savonarola, Italy, 1498.
    4. Anabaptists (Baptists) persecuted by Roman Catholics and Protestants alike.
    5. Englishmen burned at the stake:
        a. William Tyndale, Bible translator.
        b. Bishops Latimer and Ridley.
        c. Bishop Cranmer.
        d. Thomas Hawkes (for refusing to baptize his son).
    6. French Huguenots—2,000 killed in one night in the "Massacre of St. Bartholomew."
D. First amendment to U.S. Constitution: "Congress shall make no law concerning the establishment of religion or prohibiting the free exercise thereof."
    1. Religious freedom was not an automatic right, even in America.
        a. The Puritans, Dutch, and other early settlers opposed freedom of religion for any religion other than their own.
        b. The most liberal of all, Pennsylvania, required only that elected officials be Christian.
    2. There is much dismay over the demise of Bible reading and prayers in school, but I am thankful.
        a. My children are not required to chant Hindu prayers or learn the catechism of another faith.
        b. In church we can sing, chant, hum, or shout.
        c. The state requires no specific mode of sacrament.
        d. Spies are not monitoring my sermons.

E. The price we must pay to maintain political and religious freedom:
   1. Perhaps more armed struggles.
   2. An active, enlightened government.
   3. Constant vigilance regarding erosion of freedoms.
   4. Full freedom and justice for all our people.
   5. Full exercise of our religious responsibilities without exerting pressure for special privileges.

III. The Price of Spiritual Freedom
   A. Definition:
      1. While religious freedom is outward, spiritual freedom is inward.
      2. Religious freedom is the right to follow the faith of our choice without coercion or penalty; spiritual freedom is freedom from slavery to inward compulsions and restrictions.
         a. One may be physically free to worship God, but inwardly bound to oneself.
         b. One may be free to make ethical choices, but be prisoner to habits and impulses.
         c. One may be free to give to a charity, but be strapped by greed.
         d. One may be free before civil law, but guilty before God.
   B. Jesus paid the price of spiritual freedom.
      1. Scripture:
         a. "Jesus . . . endured the cross, despising the shame" (Heb. 12:2).
         b. "Redeem" and "ransom," are often used to describe what Christ did; they mean "to buy back," or "purchase at a cost."
      2. Our spiritual freedom did not come cheaply.
         a. Price of leaving heaven to come to earth.
         b. Price of betrayal, denial, and mock trial.
         c. Price of physical crucifixion and death.
   C. We must also pay a price.
      1. The small price of faith and acceptance (John 1:12).
      2. The larger price of exercising our new freedom.

Conclusion
   A. Today we celebrate freedom—political, religious, and spiritual.
   B. Let us do two things:
      1. Remember and be thankful for the price that has been paid for us.
      2. Resolve to continue paying the price to maintain these freedoms for ourselves and for our children.

Labor Day

Four Ways to Make Work More Rewarding

Scripture: II Thessalonians 3

Text: "Now such persons we command and exhort in the Lord Jesus Christ to do their work in quietness and to earn their own living" (II Thess. 3:12).

Introduction

    A. We are all acquainted with the initials TGIF, "Thank God It's Friday."

        1. This can be a positive statement: sincere thanks for Saturday's recreation and Sunday's worship.

        2. More often it is negative: meant to belittle work.

    B. The Christian perspective can make work more rewarding in the four following ways.

I. My Desire and Ability to Work Are Part of God's Image in Me

    A. Work was part of God's original creative plan.

        1. Physical work: "The Lord God took the man and put him in the garden of Eden to till it and keep it" (Gen. 2:15).

        2. Mental work: "The man gave names to all cattle, and to the birds of the air, and to every beast of the field" (Gen. 2:20).

    B. Sin has turned work into drudgery.

        1. "In the sweat of your face you shall eat bread" (Gen. 3:19).

        2. In the next generation, sin caused a labor dispute (Cain and Abel).

        3. The battle for bread is still a struggle.

        4. Conflicts, strikes, and animosities continue.

    C. We were created in God's image; we were created to work.

        1. We are God's hands, feet, muscles, and minds.

        2. Much of His creative activity is completed through us.

        3. God does not, by Himself, plow a field, write a poem, build a house, or cook a meal.

        4. Jesus, the perfect man, worked.

II. Work Is My Duty

    A. The Bible stresses the duty of work.

        1. "Six days you shall labor..." (Exod. 20:9).

        2. "Let the thief no longer steal, but rather let him labor, doing honest work with his hands" (Eph. 4:28).

3. "If any one will not work, let him not eat" (II Thess. 3:10).
4. Our text:
    a. These were Christian freeloaders, praising God for His wonderful care, but "living in idleness."
    b. Paul says, "Get to work!"
B. What about special cases?
    1. The retired:
        a. They have worked to earn their retirement.
        b. Many can continue to work as volunteers.
    2. The independently wealthy:
        a. They have no right to be idle; they should make a contribution to society.
        b. Example: the Kennedys and Rockefellers.
    3. Students and children:
        a. Learning is their work.
        b. All should be assigned certain tasks.
    4. The maimed and handicapped:
        a. Biblical reference is to those who "will not work," not those who "cannot work."
        b. The welfare system should encourage work rather than discourage it.
C. In most cases, work enables us to enjoy the necessities and even the luxuries of life with a clear conscience.

III. God Is My Employer
A. The Bible stresses that work is God-centered.
    1. "Whatever your task, work heartily, as serving the Lord and not men, knowing that from the Lord you will receive the inheritance as your reward" (Col. 3:23).
    2. Joseph, no matter what the circumstance, worked as a man who was serving God: as son, as slave, as prisoner, and as ruler.
B. Benefits of this attitude:
    1. Overcomes disappointment when others don't acknowledge the worth of our work.
    2. Gives us pride in what we do well, knowing that God knows and cares.
    3. Encourages us to be faithful in work, even when conditions are not exactly to our liking.

IV. Work Must Not Obscure the Ultimate Purpose of My Life
A. Scripture:
    1. "You shall have no other gods before me" (Exod. 20:3).
        a. An idol is anything that keeps us from God.
        b. Work can be a form of idolatry.
    2. Jesus' parable of the rich fool (Luke 12:13-21).

        a. His sin was believing that accumulating goods is the ultimate purpose in life.

    3. Incident of the rich young ruler (Luke 18:18–30).

        a. He led a good moral life.

        b. But he gave up the kingdom rather than lose his possessions.

B. Work and its results are not the supreme purpose of life.

    1. We are soul as well as body, creatures of eternity.

    2. Spiritual hunger is not satisfied by mere possessions.

    3. The very best thing in life—salvation—is free (Eph. 2:8, 9).

    4. A well-balanced life strives to meet both material and spiritual needs.

Conclusion

These, then, are four biblical ways of making our work more rewarding:

    1. My desire and ability to work are part of God's image in me.

    2. Work is my duty.

    3. God is my employer.

    4. Work must not obscure the ultimate purpose of my life.

Opening of School

The School of Small Tasks

Scripture: Jeremiah 12:1–6
Text: "If you have raced with men on foot, and they have wearied you, how will you compete with horses? And if in a safe land you fall down, how will you do in the jungle of the Jordan?" (Jer. 12:5).

Introduction

    A. Youth is a time for dreaming, especially in summer.

        1. You are anticipating the opening of school.

        2. You are probably daydreaming about the future.

            a. Dating, engagement, or marriage.

            b. Winning a football championship, becoming a doctor, writing a best seller, or going into business.

    B. Keep on daydreaming.

        1. Set your sights on the difficult and even the impossible.

        2. Determine goals, standards, and ambitions.

        3. The world needs people who think big.

    C. But I also remind you of the words God spoke to Jeremiah:

        1. (See text.)

        2. In other words, you've got to be able to master the small tasks before you can tackle the big ones.

I. God Trains Us for Big Tasks by First Giving Us Small Ones

    A. This principle restated:

        1. We've got to be able to handle the small tasks before we can even consider the large ones.

        2. We must learn to walk before we can run.

        3. We must graduate from the school of small responsibilities before entering the school of large ones.

        4. Our future success depends very much on our use of present opportunities.

    B. This process is true on all levels of life.

        1. Academic education proceeds from kindergarten to elementary, junior high, high school, college, and beyond.

        2. Vocational competence begins with training, then apprenticeship, a job, and advancements.

        3. Male-female relationships begin with mixed play and work groups, dating, and then marriage.

    C. In almost all cases, the initial steps have much to do with ultimate success.

1. How well we "run against horses" depends on how well we "run against men."
2. How well we walk through the jungle depends on how well we walk on the beach.

II. **Applications**

A. School work:
   1. You wish to do well on semester exams.
   2. So you must be attentive in class, take notes, do homework, meet every deadline, and learn study skills.

B. Sports:
   1. You may dream of being a basketball, track, football, or baseball star.
   2. But you must first show up at every practice session, learn the fundamentals, do warm-up exercises, and spend hundreds of grueling hours in practice.

C. Vocations:
   1. You anticipate success in the field of your choice.
   2. But you must begin by studying, developing basic skills, becoming dependable and responsible in small tasks, and respecting authority.

D. Marriage:
   1. You anticipate a fulfilling and happy marriage.
   2. Begin by learning to relate to the opposite sex, becoming sympathetic and understanding, establishing moral standards, and becoming financially responsible.

E. Personal stability:
   1. You anticipate being able to cope with serious illness, bereavement, financial loss, and stress.
   2. So you must begin now to deal maturely with competetive defeats, illness, and personal disappointments.

F. Religion:
   1. You anticipate a vital vibrant faith that will endure in all circumstances.
   2. So begin now with a basic commitment to Christ. Establish patterns of devotion and prayer, habits of regular worship and education, and standards of honesty and integrity. Select Christian friends. Seek answers to unresolved problems, and put your faith to work at home, school, sports, and recreation.

Conclusion

A. All of us are somewhere in the school of small tasks.
   1. Some are in the elementary grades; others are more advanced.
   2. All our present experiences are a training for the future.

B. Let us resolve, with God's help, to succeed at each level.

Thanksgiving

Coping with Prosperity

Scripture: Philippians 4:1–13
Text: "I know how to be abased, and I know how to abound; in any and all circumstances I have learned the secret of facing plenty and hunger, abundance and want" (Phil. 4:12).

Introduction

    A. Knowing how to be "abased" is not easy.
        1. Living in poverty is difficult.
        2. Coping with adversity takes courage and perseverence.
    B. Knowing how to "abound" seems much easier.
        1. Good crops and pay raises seldom bring trauma.
        2. Christian magazines seldom run articles on "How I Learned to Live with an Unexpected Inheritance."
    C. Yet, coping successfully with prosperity may be more difficult in some ways than coping with poverty.
        1. Prosperity can make us:
            a. Insensitive to the needs and rights of others.
            b. Conceited and proud.
            c. Greedy.
            d. Thankless.
        2. "It is easier," said Jesus, "for a camel to go through the eye of a needle than for a rich man to enter the kingdom of God" (Matt. 19:24).
        3. The following suggestions will help us be less endangered by prosperity.

I. Become Aware of the Abundance of Our Possessions

    A. A schoolgirl was asked to write an essay on the poor. She wrote, "Daddy is poor. Mommy is poor. Jimmy and I are poor. Our poodle is poor. Our maid is poor. Our gardener is poor..."
    B. We must get over our poverty complex.
        1. Stop confusing overspending with underearning.
        2. Start comparing ourselves to the 90% who have less rather than to the 10% who have more.

II. Take Care of God's Good Earth

    A. "The earth is the Lord's and the fulness thereof" (Ps. 24:1).
    B. We can take care of earth by:
        1. Not polluting our streams, our earth, or our waters with poisonous wastes.

2. Not defacing our world with beverage cans, paper wrappers, or plastic containers.
3. Not despoiling the earth and its beauty in the race for prosperity.

III. Trust in God, Not in Things
A. The parable of the foolish farmer (Luke 12:13–21), "Seek first his kingdom and his righteousness" (Matt. 6:33).
B. Our eternal security rests in our relationship with God, not in stocks, bonds, and property.
C. What we believe and how we live is more important than what we own.

IV. Learn Not to Overspend
A. "Where your treasure is, there will your heart be also" (Matt. 6:21).
B. Signs of the times:
  1. A wallet that holds thirty-two credit cards.
  2. Advertising aimed at snob appeal and prestige.
  3. Easy credit, low down-payments, long-term payments.
C. If we make $10,000 per year and spend $10,500, we're unhappy; if we make $35,000 and spend $35,500, we're also unhappy.

V. Share with Others
A. "Every one to whom much is given, of him will much be required" (Luke 12:48).
  1. Privilege always obligates.
  2. Responsibility increases with prosperity.
B. We are vital links in God's chain of providence.
  1. It's an honor to be part of God's distribution plan.
  2. We can't ignore the cries of human need.
C. We can do three things:
  1. We can provide immediate relief with food, clothing, etc.
  2. We can work toward an economic system which provides adequate worldwide distribution.
  3. We can strive to overcome any practice which discriminates on the basis of race, sex, nationality, or religion.

VI. Receive with Thanks
A. "For everything created by God is good, and nothing is to be rejected if it is received with thanksgiving; for then it is consecrated by the word of God and prayer" (I Tim. 4:4, 5).
  1. The Scriptures do not teach asceticism.
  2. We are not obligated to feel guilty about owning things and enjoying some of life's pleasures.
  3. We can accept these good things with a clear conscience if we are truly thankful for them.

B. Thankfulness is vitally important.
   1. The truly thankful person acknowledges his dependence on God and others.
   2. The truly thankful person cannot become conceited and self-centered.
   3. The truly thankful person cannot regard his possessions as gods.
   4. The truly thankful person cannot be discontented with what he has.

Conclusion
   A. If poverty is in our future, may we be able to cope with it.
   B. If prosperity is in our future, may we be able to cope with that too.

Christmas

Is God Like Santa Claus?

Scripture: Romans 3:21–31
Text: "They are justified by his grace as a gift, through the redemption which is in Christ Jesus" (Rom. 3:24).

Introduction

    A. Is God like Santa Claus? The question *seems* silly.
    B. Santa, in many ways, is like God.
        1. Omnipresent (on every streetcorner; travels the entire globe in one night).
        2. Omniscient ("He sees you when you're sleeping").
        3. Moral judge ("Gonna find out who's naughty and nice").
        4. Supernatural helpers (flying reindeer).
    C. Santa comes close to being the god of Christmas.
    D. But our chief concern is the opposite: God is thought by many to be like Santa Claus.

I. Santa's Presence and God's Presence

    A. Santa's presence.
        1. Visits his children one day of the year; spends 364 days in white place called North Pole.
        2. Secretly watching and keeping record, but gives no help in daily life.
    B. Many have similar idea about God's presence.
        1. Old man with long white beard, lives in white place called heaven.
        2. He is more or less keeping record of things, but is not present and active in our lives.
    C. The real God is present and active.
        1. He is no less present in one place than another.
        2. Jesus promised that the Holy Spirit would be ever-present.
        3. We are commanded to keep in communication with God.
        4. God doesn't want to be just a Christmas and Easter god.

II. Santa's Believability and God's Believability

    A. Santa's believability.
        1. Belief in Santa is supposed to be for childhood only.
        2. Sooner or later children find out he's not real.

3. They discover parents are playing a game (a fun game, but nevertheless a game).
    a. Parents are telling the child something they, themselves, don't believe.
    b. Lesson: faith is something you outgrow.
4. When they become parents, these children will teach Santa to their children, and the cycle continues.
B. Many have a similar idea about God's believability.
    1. Common phrase: "Christmas is for children."
    2. Implications:
        a. Christmas is not for adults.
        b. Faith is meant to be outgrown.
        c. Belief is just a pleasant experience of childhood.
        d. Luke 2 is reduced to the level of a Rudolph the reindeer story.
C. The real God is the Lord of all of life.
    1. Believe in Him as your Savior, not as a sentimental childhood story.
    2. Christ is for adult and child, male and female, rich and poor.
    3. He who endures to the end will be saved (see II Tim. 2:11, 12).

III. Santa's Standards of Judgment and God's Standards of Judgment
A. Santa's standards:
    1. Keeps a record and gives gifts accordingly (a kind of "works salvation").
    2. Children discover that it doesn't really happen that way.
        a. No matter how they act, they receive the gifts anyway.
        b. Santa's judgments are idle threats.
B. Many have a similar idea about God's judgments.
    1. Many people believe in a "works salvation."
    2. But they don't believe God is very strict.
        a. He blusters a lot, but doesn't enforce.
        b. He threatens with hell, but won't send anybody there.
C. The real God is a holy God.
    1. Consider Isaiah's vision (Isa. 6:1-5).
    2. "God is not mocked, for whatever a man sows, that he will also reap" (Gal. 6:7).
    3. Many "Santa Claus sermons" are preached at funerals.
    4. We must return to a healthy fear of God (Ps. 111:10).
D. God saves by forgiving, not by forgetting.
    1. God conquered evil, not by pretending it wasn't there, but by sending Christ to deal with it.

45

2. Exposition of Romans 3:23-26:
    a. "All have sinned" is a realistic appraisal of mankind (v. 23).
    b. We don't earn our salvation; consider "grace" and "gift" (v. 24).
    c. Salvation is paid for by Christ; see "redemption" and "expiation" (vv. 24b, 25).
    d. Salvation is received by faith (v. 25).
    e. Thus, God found a way to be both holy and loving (v. 26).

Conclusion
A. God isn't like Santa Claus.
B. His Christmas gift is not dependent on who is "naughty or nice."
C. His gift is already paid for and is the most expensive gift.
D. It is available to all who will receive it by faith.
E. Faith is not a childhood pleasantry, but a total lifetime commitment.

Sometimes It's Better to Receive Than to Give

Scripture: John 1:1-18
Text: "But to all who received him, who believed in his name, he gave power to become children of God" (John 1:12).

Introduction
1. Jesus said, "It is more blessed to give than to receive" (Acts 20:35).
2. That's generally true—but not always.
3. It's sometimes better to receive than to give.
4. Here are four reasons why receiving is sometimes more vital than giving.

I. Gracious Receiving Honors the Giver
A. This is true when Christmas gifts are opened.
    1. The delight of a boy finding a train under the tree is surpassed by the delight of his father in watching him.
    2. The same is true of many other gifts.
B. Refusing to accept a gift is a worse insult than failing to give a gift.
C. We please God by receiving His Christmas gift.

1. God's Christmas gift was refused by Jesus' own countrymen (v. 11).
2. The joy of a sinner who repents is exceeded only by the joy of the angels (Luke 15:10).
3. God's greatest joy is being able to share with us His life, His salvation, and His heaven.

II. We Can Give Only If We Have First Received

A. We can't give away anything we don't have, and in order to have, we must first receive.
   1. Teachers must receive knowledge in order to share it.
   2. People who have received love are most capable of sharing love.
   3. Scripture references:
      a. John the Baptist could "bear witness to the light" because he had received it (v. 8).
      b. Paul said, "For I delivered to you as of first importance what I also received" (I Cor. 15:3).
B. Unless you have received comfort from God, you cannot give God's comfort to others.
   1. Unless you have received God's life, you cannot share that life with your neighbor.
   2. Unless you have faith, you cannot share that faith with your children.

III. It Often Takes More Character to Receive Than to Give

A. This may sound strange in an era of consumer fraud, welfare fraud, embezzlement, and robbery.
B. Receiving requires humility.
   1. The publican, who was humble, went to his house justified, but the Pharisee was too proud to receive grace.
   2. It takes humility to accept advice, direction, or criticism.
C. Receiving requires trust.
   1. We are often suspicious of a "free" offer (usually with good reason).
   2. People also tend to be suspicious when God offers something free; they would prefer to work for it.

IV. Receiving Is the Only Way of Obtaining God's Christmas Gift

A. "But to all who received him, who believed on his name, he gave power to become children of God" (John 1:12).
B. Every Christmas gift is paid for; Christ paid for this one.
C. If we try to purchase or earn God's gift, we will not obtain it.
   1. We cannot earn it by baptism or church membership.
   2. We cannot pay for it by giving stained glass windows,

serving on committees, teaching Sunday school, or even trying to live a good life.

D. We must accept God's Christmas gift by a deliberate act of the will.

Conclusion

A. It's sometimes better to receive than to give because:
   1. Gracious receiving honors the giver.
   2. We can give only if we have first received.
   3. It often takes more character to receive than to give.
   4. Receiving is the only way of obtaining God's Christmas gift.

B. May this Christmas be a time of receiving as well as giving.